DUNGEONS, GALLOWS AND SEVERED HEADS OF London

First published in 2002 by Watling St Publishing
The Old Chapel
East End
Northleach
Gloucestershire
GL54 3PQ

Printed in Thailand

Copyright © Watling St Publishing Ltd 2002

ISBN 1-904153-03-8

24681097531

Cover design and illustration: Mark Davis
Cartoons: Martin Angel

DUNGEONS, GALLOWS AND SEVERED HEADS OF London

Travis Elborough

WATLING STREET

Travis Elborough is a freelance writer and lives in North London. He likes playing football but hates pasta.

This book is for Lauren

Contents

Introduction   7

1 Bloody Beginnings   9

2 Storming Norman   14

3 Tales of Terror from the Tower 22

4 Slaughter at Smithfield   40

5 The Killing of the King   50

6 Nasty Newgate   54

7 The Golden Age of the Gallows 68

8 Ready for Reform   85

Gory Place to Visit   93

Capital Punishment!

For hundreds of years London wasn't just England's capital city – it was the city of capital punishment! Being locked up or having your head lopped off was once part of everyday life in old London town - just like overcrowded tubes are today (and only slightly more unpleasant!)

Most tourist attractions tend to be the nice buildings, pretty statues and the magnificent museums. In this book we'll be exploring the nastier side of the city's history. We'll take a peek at the hideous dungeons that lurked beneath the ground. We'll go in search of the grim gallows and gruesome gaols that used to dominate the city. We'll meet murderous monarchs, cruel killers and vicious villains. We'll discover rotten rules and painful punishments and come face to face with severed heads and horrible hangings.

Old London's narrow streets teemed with dark deeds and bloody murders. Until the 1700s there wasn't even a police force to protect the city. Londoners were guarded by local watchmen – a bit like today's Neighbourhood Watch schemes, but a million times more hopeless. Crooks had little to fear from them but if they were caught they faced brutal punishments or death. And justice really was rough. If the city was a dangerous place, the royal palaces were hardly safer. For centuries England's kings and queens could execute almost anyone who annoyed them and, as we shall see, they really were a bloody bunch.

Let's begin by turning back the clock and seeing just how bad London's good old days were.

Don't lose your head!

CHAPTER ONE

Bloody Beginnings

The Romans founded London. Julius Caesar first landed in Britain in 55BC but the Romans didn't invade until 43AD. By 60AD they had established a port on the banks of the Thames. They called it Londinium. Unfortunately halfway through building defences at Southwark, they were attacked by angry Ancient Britons. The Iceni tribe from East Anglia led by the warrior Queen Boudicca razed Londinium to the ground. They burnt, crucified and hanged all of the city's inhabitants. Not a good start for London but a hint of things to come …

When in Londinium

The Romans rebuilt Londinium and for over 300 years it prospered. But after all this time the Romans got bored. They had built thousands of straight roads, created hundreds of great cities and invented central heating. What else was there for them to do? They took longer and longer baths, lazed about eating grapes and drank more and more wine.

When hoards of hairy Barbarians from Germany started attacking them they were completely unprepared. The Roman Empire collapsed and tribes from Germany – the Angles, Jutes and Saxons – swarmed into Britain.

The Saxon city

The Saxons took control of London. They gave it a new name – Ludenwic (wic is Old English for port). They built new, crooked roads and houses. In fact today's London owes more to the Saxons than to the Romans. Many of their laws lasted until the Middle Ages. The Saxon kings had their court at Westminster – now the home of our lawmakers in the Houses of Parliament.

Anglo-Saxon law and order

Anglo-Saxon justice was harsh. Wrongdoers could face a number of revolting disfigurements or deaths. Limbs were chopped off, noses sliced from faces and eyes put out.

Executions were nasty. The condemned were throttled, burned, drowned, buried alive, stoned or thrown off cliffs. Anyone who claimed to be innocent had to take a test or ordeal to prove it. These ordeals were horrible too.

The ordeal by fire

The accused would have to walk for nine paces carrying a red-hot iron bar.

Afterwards their hands were examined. If they had not burned they were judged innocent. Otherwise they were declared guilty and executed.

The ordeal by water

The accused would be thrown into the Thames. If they sank, they were found to be innocent, but if they floated, they were guilty – and then fished out and killed. Either way, it was curtains.

Viking vengeance

At the turn of the eighth century vicious Vikings from Denmark began attacking Britain. In 870 AD they sacked London, massacring almost everyone who lived there.

Alfred the Great, the King of Wessex, decided to fight back. He recaptured London in 886. Under his reign new and more civilized laws were introduced. The ordeals stayed but gruesome punishments or death could be avoided by paying compensation.

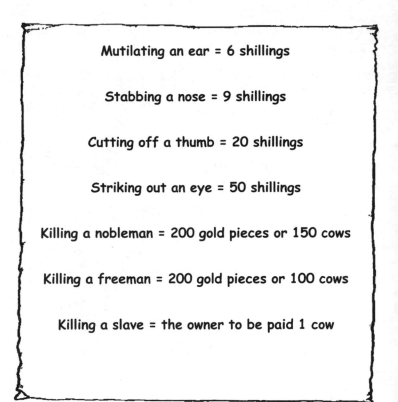

Mutilating an ear = 6 shillings

Stabbing a nose = 9 shillings

Cutting off a thumb = 20 shillings

Striking out an eye = 50 shillings

Killing a nobleman = 200 gold pieces or 150 cows

Killing a freeman = 200 gold pieces or 100 cows

Killing a slave = the owner to be paid 1 cow

If you were unable to pay the fine you were taken as a slave. If you refused to pay or tried to escape the accuser was allowed to kill you.

Anglo-Saxon rule came to an end in 1066 when the Frenchman William of Normandy – later called William the Conqueror - defeated King Harold at the Battle of Hastings. (An arrow hit Harold in the eye. Ouch!) From Hastings William marched to London. He set fire to Southwark and was promptly let into the city without a fight. On Christmas Day he was crowned king of England at Westminster Abbey. Kings and queens of England have been crowned there ever since.

During William's coronation his guards - who only spoke French - thought the cheering English crowds were insulting their master. To punish them they burnt all the houses in the neighbourhood.

CHAPTER TWO

Storming Norman

William the Conqueror was also known as William the Bastard because he was illegitimate (his parents had never married). It was a very fitting nickname. William was extremely unpleasant. He was vastly overweight; so fat that people joked about him being pregnant. He was a cruel and merciless ruler. Shortly after taking the throne a rebellion against him broke out in the north of England. William ordered whole towns to be burned down and had the rebels slaughtered.

For the chop

William found hanging dull. So in 1075 he had Walthoef the Earl of Northumberland beheaded. England's very first severed head. Soon all the lords demanded to have their heads chopped off. They didn't want to be strangled like peasants. Beheading was French; it was the cool and stylish way to die.

William also loved to maim criminals. He thought killing them was a waste of manpower. A crook with their nose mangled could be put to work on the land. It also

helped remind the grubby English that he was the boss. He was the first king to think of using punishments to deter crime.

The tower of power

To keep control of London, William built a fortress beside the river Thames. Its location was perfect. It was protected by an old Roman wall on one side and by the river on the other. From here William could spot any invaders and keep an eye on the city. His fortress – the Tower of London - dominated the landscape. It was a sign of his power.

Originally the Tower was made of wood. With William's fondness for burning buildings this wasn't very wise. In 1078 it was rebuilt in stone. The imposing wooden castle was then transformed into a magnificent royal palace. The Tower housed the king and his barons, the army and the royal mint (the place where coins are cast). There were stables for horses and it even had its own farm - with pigs and chickens for the king's table and a patch of land for growing vegetables. It must have got pretty smelly in there.

William doesn't appear to have used the Tower as a prison or had anyone executed there. That soon changed, however.

Time for the Tower

William died fighting in France. He fell off his horse while trying to burn down a castle and burst his bladder. His son, also called William, took the English throne. He was even more unpleasant than his father was. He had ginger hair and so he was nicknamed Rufus - Latin for red. Everyone hated him. Fortunately he was killed by a stray arrow while hunting in the New Forest. (He was probably murdered.) His brother Henry seized the crown.

Prisoner Number 1

King Henry I promptly arrested Rufus's right-hand man – Rannulf Flambard, the Bishop of Durham. Rannulf was locked in the Tower. He was its first prisoner and also the first person to escape.

Rannulf, however, wasn't flung into a hideous dank dungeon. He had a nice set of rooms. He had his own servants and was allowed any luxuries he wanted. It was more like a hotel than a prison. After six months though he was pretty fed up and decided to escape by getting a rope smuggled into the fortress. He then got his guards drunk, and using the rope, he clambered to freedom.

A few years later one prisoner tried the same thing and came to a very nasty end. Griffin, the portly Prince of Wales, was so fat that the rope he was using to escape snapped. He plummeted headfirst into the ground below.

From Rannulf onwards the tower became notorious as the King's special prison.

Accommodation at the Tower was by rank. If you were a king or prince you could still live like one behind its walls. King John II of France, who was captured by Edward III in 1356, had his own team of cooks. He thought British food was disgusting.

Prisoners had to pay for their cells. Nobles were allowed to have their own servants but they had to pay extra for them.

Prison Fees per week in the 1300s

A Duke = £3	**A chaplain** = 6 shillings
An Earl = £2	**A gentleman** = 6 shillings
A baron = £1	**A yeoman** = 3 shillings
A knight = 10 shillings	**Any other servant** = 3 shillings

Poorer prisoners or people the king or queen really didn't liked wound up in the Tower's damp dungeons. These had no windows and were constantly being flooded by the Thames. Chained and manacled, these unfortunate prisoners lived in total darkness.

It was rare for people to languish in the Tower for long. Most were only being held there until they could be executed.

English executions

Henry I not only turned the Tower of London into the royal prison, he also introduced the death penalty for the theft of anything worth more than 6 pence. (He was a bit of a miser with money.)

Henry's successors greatly increased the numbers of executions. They also came up with new and even more gruesome ways to kill their subjects.

Theft, murder, arson, burglary, highway robbery, hunting the king or queen's deer, cutting down the king or queen's trees and treason (betraying or sometimes just annoying the king or queen) were all punishable by death.

Nobles were normally executed by having their heads chopped off by an axe. Ordinary people had to make do with being hanged. It was thought indecent to see women swinging by the neck so they were strangled and then burned. Heretics – those who disagreed with the Church - were burned alive. Drowning was also popular. The Baron of Baynard Castle at Blackfriars used to drown traitors in the Thames. A grim variation was invented for sailors. Any sailor caught stealing ropes or nets faced a terrible death. Their tongues were pulled out with pincers and their throats were cut. After this mutilation their hands and feet were tied together and they were then tossed into the Thames at low tide. As the tide rose

they drowned, the water gushing into their lungs through the gaping holes in their necks. (Urrghh!)

The hideous slaughter: hang, draw and quarter

In 1241 King Henry III invented a new and excruciating way to execute anyone that got on his nerves.

Henry was fed up with lords and barons misbehaving. How was he supposed to keep the plebs in order when the nobles were constantly trying to seize his throne? The final straw came when a young nobleman, William Maurice, was found guilty of piracy and treason. Henry thought beheading was just too good for him. A couple of chops of an axe and it would all be over. Why should William, a jumped-up little oik, receive such a swift and painless death? Surely there must be a more painful and humiliating way for him to die? The King scratched his head, tugged at his beard and came up with an ingeniously awful way to execute him.

For starters he had William dragged or 'drawn' by horses to the execution site. (Falling over and grazing a knee can be painful but imagine having your whole body scraped along the ground!) Arriving battered and bleeding, William was then hanged on a scaffold until he was nearly dead. At this point he was cut down. Gasping for breath he could only look on in horror as the executioner strode toward him. Before his very eyes the executioner sliced his stomach open. William's guts were yanked out on to the floor and the pulp of gory innards set on fire. William died in agony inhaling the acrid fumes of his own burning flesh. His body was then cut into four pieces. Each bit was coated with tar and exhibited on London Bridge as a warning to others. Henry was delighted. He called this method of execution hanging, drawing and quartering. His son Edward thought it was brilliant too. When he became King Edward I in 1272 he made it the main punishment for treason.

The benefit of books or how reading really could save your life

The one group of people who didn't have to worry about the death penalty were monks and vicars. Only the church could try priests and the church was much more lenient than the king and his courts. Vicars found guilty of manslaughter or stealing

were branded – the nasty practice of burning a mark on to the skin with a red-hot iron. If they offended again they were executed but at least there was one chance of avoiding the axe or the gallows.

If a naughty vicar wound up in front of a criminal court he had to prove that he was a priest to get off. To do this he had to read a passage from the Bible - part of the 51st Psalm. This was called the Benefit of Clergy. This lucky legal loophole was soon extended to anyone who could read. Some people just learnt the verse by heart to avoid the gallows! There were certain crimes like highway robbery, treason and heresy where it couldn't be used. As time went on the list increased until it was of little help but for 400 years it was the only compassion offered to wrongdoers.

CHAPTER THREE

Tales of Terror from the Tower

The horrendous hanging of London's Jews

Our first tale is one of the darkest moments in the Tower's and England's history; it is the hideous Holocaust - a mass murder - of over 600 London Jews.

A community of Jews had first come to London soon after the Norman Conquest - William the Conqueror and his son Rufus had encouraged Jews from Normandy to join them in England.

Londoners disliked the newcomers on sight. What did these strangers want? Why did they dress and talk differently? 'It was bad enough being ruled by the French,' they moaned, 'but Jews as well ... whatever next?' The city officials agreed. They decided to prevent Jews from opening businesses or running market stalls. As Christian merchants were prevented from lending money, the Jews were allowed to work as bankers. The area they settled in – recorded now by the street name Old Jewry – became London's financial centre, as it still is today.

As they thrived the resentment grew. Londoners who had gladly borrowed money from them hated having to pay it back.

If they were short of cash they grumbled about the Jews, conveniently forgetting that money-lending was all that the community could do.

In King John's reign anti-Jewish feeling boiled over. In 1215 an angry mob stormed into London's Jewish quarter. They set fire to houses, looted banks and beat up anyone who stood in their way. For a while the Jews had to hide in the Tower for safety.

When King Edward I took the throne from Henry II in 1272 he was heavily in debt and very unpopular. He wanted cash and adoration, and he wanted it quickly. Who was currently hated more than he was? Who had more money than he did? The Jews. He knew that if he lined his big, royal pockets with money from the Jews it was much more likely to boost his popularity than damage it.

He imposed new taxes on them and took away their right to own land. Chillingly he passed a law forcing all Jews over the age of seven to wear a yellow patch on their clothes. (In the twentieth century Hitler and the Nazis in Germany did almost the same thing.) Branded in this way they felt more like cattle than human beings. The yellow patches made them an easy target for attacks.

In 1278 Edward cooked up another scheme.

He falsely accused the Jews of forging coins. His troops dragged over 600 Jews from their homes. Paraded through the city they were pelted with rotten food and spat on by jeering bystanders. Edward cast them into the bowels of the Tower, into his most rancid dungeon. Now it was a foul prison. They had been loyal English subjects and begged to be able to prove their innocence. Their pleas fell on deaf ears. Edward had over 260 Jews hanged. Of the remainder hundreds starved to death in the putrid royal dungeons. Others were brutally tortured and horrifically murdered by their gaolers.

Twelve years later Edward expelled all of the remaining Jews from England. They did not return until the time of Oliver Cromwell some 300 years later.

Dick Dastardly and the Princes in the Tower

History has not been kind to King Richard III. William Shakespeare portrayed him as an evil scheming hunchback. Some people think this is a bit unfair and argue that Richard was actually a great ruler. He may well have been a 'good' king but he was a terrible babysitter. While he was looking after his two nephews they mysteriously disappeared.

When King Edward IV died in 1483 the crown passed to his thirteen-year-old son Edward. ('Edward' was King Edward IV's favourite name.) As Edward was just a teenager a guardian or protector was appointed to take care of him. Richard (Edward IV's brother and then just plain old Richard of Gloucester) got the job. He was staying at the Tower of London at the time and invited the Duke of Hastings round for dinner. Hastings was young Edward's tutor and had been one of Edward IV's closest friends.

Hastings made his way to the Tower, his stomach rumbling in anticipation. (He'd skipped lunch to make room for the sumptuous banquet he expected to receive.) He was met by Richard and a couple of the burliest looking waiters he'd ever seen. Something didn't seem quite right about all this.

'Ah, sorry, Richard – am I too early?' asked Hastings.

'No, just a bit overdressed,' replied Richard.

'In what way?'

'Your head. It's still on your shoulders. I won't eat my tea until it's been removed.'

With that Hastings was seized by the 'waiters' and dragged on to Tower Green. He was beheaded over a lump of timber that had been discarded by a carpenter. Hastings was the first person to be beheaded on Tower Green.

With Hastings out of the way, Richard moved Edward and his little brother, Richard, who was nine years old, into the Tower.

The boys might have looked forward to staying with their Uncle Richard. The Tower was an exciting place. It was a regal palace full of grand courtiers, soldiers and teams of servants. It had its own zoo and an archery range. The last time that the princes appeared in  public they were spotted playing contentedly in the Tower's grounds.

With the princes safely tucked away, Richard craftily had himself crowned the King of England. Within weeks of his coronation the princes simply vanished from the Tower never to be seen again. Had Richard 'taken care of them' by having them murdered? What really happened to them remains a mystery but ...

30 years after their sinister disappearance Sir Thomas More wrote a book about Richard. In it Thomas claimed that Richard ordered his crony Sir James Tyrell to kill them. James didn't want to gets his hands dirty so he hired a couple of thugs to do it for him. The thugs, Mr Green and Mr Forest, smothered the poor boys to death with pillows and then buried them in the tower.

But can we believe Thomas's story? Thomas had worked for Henry Tudor (King Henry VII), the man who knocked Richard off the throne. Thomas needed the approval of Henry Tudor's son, King Henry VIII. (Without it Thomas himself would have ended up in the Tower for writing the book.) So surprise, surprise, Richard turns out to be a nasty old murderer while Henry Tudor is the dashing saviour of England. (Umm, I wonder ...)

In the 1680s the skeletons of two boys were discovered buried under a staircase in the White Tower. The mystery appeared to be solved – the princes had been murdered, as More had claimed. However, scientists who examined the bones in the 1930s could not prove that they definitely belonged to the princes.

Some believe the princes were not murdered at all but were smuggled out of the Tower. There is even a rumour that the younger prince, Richard of York, can be seen in a painting of Thomas More and his family!

If they were murdered, is Richard really the only suspect?

Richard was a ruthless murderer but Henry Tudor had just as many reasons for wanting the princes out of the way. A dozen or more people had a better claim to the throne than Henry. Young Edward posed a real threat to his reign. Could Henry, rather than Richard, have murdered them? Or did he spare their lives but force them to live secretly with his trusted friend Thomas?

We just don't know.

Harmful Henry VIII

Henry VIII is most famous for having had six wives and executing two of them. It wasn't only members of his own family that he killed; Henry had over 70,000 people executed. He was king for thirty-eight years, which means that on average he had five people killed every day! (Nice one, Henry.)

Henry's craze for executions only really kicked off after he had made himself head of the Church of England. Henry desperately wanted a son to rule after him but his first wife, Catherine of Aragon, had given birth to a daughter, Mary. He decided a new queen was needed. Henry started dating Anne Boleyn, who was one of Catherine's maids. He asked the Pope if he could divorce Catherine and marry Anne. The Pope refused. Henry was used to getting his own way. (He was the King, after all!) If the Pope and his Catholic Church wouldn't give him a divorce then, stuff it! he'd create his own Church.

Hundreds of priests, monks and nuns who refused to accept Henry's new Protestant Church were put to death. Suspects were sometimes gruesomely tortured to obtain confessions. The dungeons in the Tower had a rack (a barbaric stretching device that pulls the body apart) and something even nastier called the Scavenger's Daughter. The Scavenger was a hideous crushing machine; it squeezed the prisoner, like a tube of toothpaste, until the blood spurted out of them!

Anne's Agony

In 1543 Anne Askew became the only woman ever to be racked in the Tower. Anne was a fierce critic of Henry and was arrested for heresy – the crime of insulting God and the Church. (Who ran the church? Henry, of course!) When she was taken to the Tower she refused to say anything. Two of Henry's ministers decided to torture her. They stretched her on the rack until her bones popped out of their joints. Ouch! She still didn't confess. When they untied her she fainted. Anne awoke in agony, unable to use her arms and legs. (It gets worse.) She was then carried in a chair to Smithfield and burnt at the stake as a witch.

Butchering Boleyn

After all of Henry's efforts to make sure he had a son, Anne Boleyn, his second wife, gave birth to a girl, Elizabeth. Henry became bored with Anne. He went on the prowl again. Soon he was strolling about the court with a girl called

Jane - who was anything but plain. Now all he had to do was get rid of Anne. Henry hit on a scam. He accused her of having other boyfriends and had her sentenced to death. How unfair was that? Henry had done the wandering, not Anne.

The Queen was brought by boat to the Tower. The Tower had been Anne's home - she had made the same journey along the river after her coronation – now she was being taken here to die. Anne entered through Traitor's Gate, passing an iron grille covered with festering severed heads. It was an awful hint of what was to come. A swordsman from Calais in France had been hired to carry out the execution. On 19 May 1536 Anne was led out on to Tower Green. Trembling with fear she knelt down before the swordsman. He sliced off her head with a single blow. Stingy old Henry had not bothered to buy a coffin for Anne. Her body and head were buried in an old trunk that had been used to keep arrows in. The very next day Henry announced he was going to marry Jane Seymour. (Why wait so long?)

Kill me, Cate

Six years later Henry went through the whole thing again. (Jane gave birth to a son, Edward, and then died.) He divorced his fourth wife Anne of Cleeves to marry Catherine Howard. Catherine was only eighteen years of age. Henry was now fifty-one. He was also in terrible health; he was overweight and covered in smelly sores that oozed sticky pus. Catherine was caught kissing Thomas Culpepper, a dashing young man who worked at the palace. (Can you blame her?) She was taken to the Tower and beheaded on Tower Green on 13 February 1542. Where did Henry have her buried? Right beside Anne Boleyn.

Chips off the old block

Henry would have been proud of his children. They killed almost as many people as he did. Edward, Mary and Elizabeth all had enemies chopped at the Tower

When Henry died in 1547 his nine-year-old son Edward became King. Edward VI was a very sickly little boy. He had TB (a horrible lung disease) and was ill for most of his short reign. Edward was only fifteen when he died. His uncle, Edward Seymour (why are there so many Edwards?), helped him to rule.

One night Uncle Eddie was tiptoeing about the palace when he was attacked by a guard dog. Frightened that he was going to be mauled he shot the dog. Unfortunately the mutt was the boy King's

favourite. Uncle Eddie was marched off to the Tower and his head lopped off. (Unlucky Eddie!)

Little Edward was a big fan of his Dad's Church and the new Protestant religion. By 1553 he knew he was dying. His hair and nails had all fallen out and he was spluttering up blood whenever he coughed. His half-sister Mary was next in line to the throne. Mary had remained a staunch Catholic. Edward was determined that she should not become queen. He arranged for his cousin Lady Jane Grey, who was sixteen years old, to be crowned after he died.

Lady Jane Grey reigned for just nine days before Mary grabbed the Crown from her. Jane and her hubby Guildford Dudley were flung into the Tower. Guildford was executed on Tower Hill on 12 February 1554. Guildford's bloody, headless body was wheeled passed Jane's cell window in a cart. Once the guards had disposed of Guildford they came to collect Jane. This teenage girl, who had never even asked to be Queen, had her head hacked off by an axe on Tower Green.

Queen Mary was such a murderous monarch that she was known as Bloody Mary. As she did most of her slaughtering at Smithfield we shall come back to her later (see Chapter Four – Slaughter at Smithfield).

Bloody Bess

Elizabeth I was a feisty redhead who never married. Like her grumpy old dad Henry, Bess had a short temper. Anyone who annoyed her quickly wound up in the Tower. The unluckier ones soon found themselves without heads. (These were hard times for hat makers!) Bess had over 250 Catholics executed.

During her reign Bess refused to spend a single night in the Tower. It had too many bad memories for her - her sister Mary had imprisoned her in it and her mother, Anne Boleyn, had been executed there.

Bess loved beheading but she was also keen on Edward I's grim method of execution: hanging, drawing and quartering. The Queen even ordered her executioners to make sure Catholic victims were still alive when their guts were pulled out. (I bet they were gutted!)

Beheading Bob

Robert Devereux Earl of Essex was one of Bess's favourite courtiers. Bob thought he was the bee's knees. He was young, rich and good-looking. Women swooned as he walked by, men envied him and cats longed to claw the stockings on his shapely legs.

Bess sent Bob to Ireland on a special mission. Bob hadn't wanted to go, he'd been perfectly happy lounging about in London being admired by women, men and cats. He hated Ireland and Ireland hated him. After six months he had made a complete mess of his mission. He crawled back to England and begged the Queen for forgiveness. Bess had him booted out of the palace.

Bob was so angry at being humiliated that he hatched a plot to overthrow Queen Bess. The Queen soon found out about it and had Bob arrested and imprisoned in the Tower. Bess wasted no time in sentencing her former friend to death. On 24 February Bob was led onto to Tower Green and his handsome head severed by an ugly great axe. He was the last person ever to be beheaded at the Tower.

Raleigh Good Times

Queen Elizabeth always had a soft spot for the dashing explorer Sir Walter Raleigh (the man who brought tobacco and potatoes to Britain). Bess funded his trips to America. She was enthralled by his stories of this strange new land. She marvelled at the bizarre vegetables he gave her and was astounded when he shoved twigs into his mouth and set fire to them. This still didn't stop the Queen casting him into the Tower when he married one of her ladies-in-waiting and failed to invite her to the wedding!

Walter's fortunes started to suffer after Elizabeth died and James VI of Scotland became King James I of England. James hated smoking and if there was one thing he hated even more than smoking it was Walter. Where do you think James sent Walter? Yes, you guessed it, back to the Tower.

Walter spent the next eleven years lodged in the Bloody Tower but eventually his luck ran out. James sentenced him to death in 1617. He was to be beheaded not at Tower Green but at Westminster.

Sneaky James arranged for Walter to be executed on the day of the Lord Mayor's Show. The show was a public holiday for Londoners, with parades, feasts and games. James hoped that these festivities would be more popular than Walter's execution. He was wrong. So many people gathered at Westminster's Old Palace Yard that it was difficult for Walter to actually get to the scaffold. Walter asked an old man why he had come. 'To see you. God bless you, sir,' said the man. Walter thanked him and then gave him his lace nightcap, saying, 'You have more need of it than me.'

At the scaffold Walter checked the blade and chatted to the executioner before bravely laying his head on the block. The executioner was so nervous it took him two blows to sever Walter's head. The head was then placed in a red leather bag and taken to Walter's wife. (I'm sure she'd rather have had some flowers!)

Guy Fawkes' Gentle Tortures

Every 5 November on Bonfire Night we remember
The Gunpowder Plot – the dastardly scheme to blow
up the Houses of Parliament. Guy Fawkes is the most
famous of all the conspirators but the plot was not
his idea. The plot was hatched by the radical
Catholic Robert Catesby and his friends, Thomas
Percy, Thomas Winwith and John Wright. Guy was
just the explosives expert. He was the only one who
knew how to light a fuse and set up the barrels of
powder needed to blow King James I and all his
ministers sky high. The night before Parliament was

due to open, Guy was discovered in the cellars below Whitehall. The Plot had come within hours of succeeding. Guy was taken to the Tower and lodged in one of its foulest dungeons. (The gunpowder of the plot was also taken to the Tower; it was placed in the King's storeroom.) King James himself interrogated Guy. He demanded to know who the other plotters were. Guy refused to reveal any names. James instructed his guards to begin applying the 'gentle tortures'.

The gentle tortures were not very gentle. They involved hanging Guy upside down from a wall in iron manacles. To begin with the manacles graze the skin. After a few hours they start to sever tendons in the wrists and eventually they chip into the bone. James's guards didn't wait that long. Although Guy was in agony he still would not tell them anything. More drastic methods were applied. Guy was racked. He talked.

The conspirators and anyone who had helped them were rounded up and brought to the Tower. Robert Catesby and Thomas Percy were killed resisting arrest. They got off lightly. Two men died while being tortured in the Tower. The remaining plotters met hideous deaths. They were hung, drawn and quartered at the Old Palace Yard at Westminster on 30 January 1606. They were executed by the building they had planned to destroy. (Guy, crippled by the rack, had to be carried onto the scaffold.) As a warning to others, their severed heads were put on spikes just outside the Houses of Parliament.

CHAPTER FOUR

Slaughter at Smithfield

Smithfield is now London's biggest meat market but for over 400 years it was a place of public execution. Smithfield stood just outside the old city walls. In the Middle Ages it was a large green field - 'a smooth field' - where horses, pigs, cows and chickens were bought and sold. Each year a huge festival called the Bartholomew Fair was held here. Like today's Notting Hill Carnival it was a time for dancing, eating and drinking. The field was used for royal tournaments, jousting contests and sporting events. Until the fifteenth century - when the gallows were moved to Tyburn (now Marble Arch) – most of London's criminals were executed at Smithfield. In 1305 Edward I wanted to make an example of the Scottish rebel William Wallace. He decided to execute him in a grisly public spectacle at Smithfield.

Edward had seized control of Scotland in 1296. Most of the Scottish nobles had been too busy arguing with each other to fight against him. William Wallace of Renfrew, however, was made of sterner stuff. This Braveheart, as he was nicknamed, was determined to kick these Sassenachs out of Scotland. For two years he made

Edward's life hell. His rebel army recaptured strongholds, burned down garrisons and thrashed English troops on the battlefield. Eventually, though, his forces were simply outnumbered by the English. The revolt was brutally crushed in 1298 and William went into hiding. He was captured in Glasgow seven years later – one of his own men had betrayed him. William was taken to Westminster Hall in London. Only the most awful execution would satisfy Edward. If these Scots were so fond of haggis – a dish made of sheep's lungs and livers – see how they liked having their own guts pulled out and grilled. He sentenced William to be hung, drawn and quartered.

William was tied to a team of horses and dragged all the way from Westminster to Smithfield. Along the way he was pelted with stones and rotten vegetables. By the time he arrived at Smithfield a vast crowd had gathered to witness his gruesome death. Great cheers went up when the executioner placed the noose around his neck. When his face turned blue he was cut down. While he was still alive his stomach was slit open and his intestines plucked out. These were burned in front of him. The bloodthirsty mob whooped with delight. William's agony was finally brought to an end when he was beheaded. Just to be on the safe side his body was then cut into four pieces and his head impaled on a spike at London Bridge. (Better severed than sorry!)

Wat no head?

Wat Tyler was another rebel leader who was executed at Smithfield. Wat had to make do with a dull old stabbing followed by beheading but his death ended the most extraordinary rebellion England has ever seen: The Peasants' Revolt.

In the 1300s, famine and the Black Death (a really frightful plague) had ravaged England. To make matters worse, England was also at war with France. The Hundred Years War (which weirdly lasted for 116 years) was expensive. King Edward III's minister John Legge created a new tax to pay for it. The Head (or Poll) Tax required everyone over the age of fifteen to pay the king three groats a year. The King realized that not everyone could afford that much so it was agreed that the rich in each town or borough would pay more. The trouble was that in very poor areas there were no rich people to pay extra. The poor were forced to pay more than they could afford. This was unfair and the tax was loathed.

When Edward died in 1377 his son Richard, who was only ten years old, became King. Richard relied on his uncle, John of Gaunt, to rule. Everyone hated John. He was a bully who didn't give two figs about a load of whingeing peasants. Peasants were seen by most landowners as a nuisance. Why should they pay these smelly creatures proper wages? A cow could be forced to work for scraps of food, it produced milk and when its ploughing days were over, it could be sold for meat or turned into leather.

What use was a peasant who couldn't work? By 1381, though, the whingeing peasants had had quite enough of John of Gaunt and his kind. Thousands of angry men from Kent and Essex, led by a roofer called Wat Tyler, converged on London. They were fed up with being ignored and abused. They wanted justice and they wanted it now. They demanded that the Poll Tax be abolished and they wanted an end to serfdom – the law that bound poor labourers to the land they worked on.

The men attempted to meet the King at Greenwich but Richard, who was only fourteen years old, was uneasy about landing his barge there. The rebels, annoyed by what they took as a rebuff, went on the rampage. Storming through Southwark, they set fire to the Marshalsea Prison and with the aid of Londoners made their way across London Bridge. The mob gained entrance to the Tower of London and to their delight discovered the hated Archbishop of Canterbury, Simon Sudbury, and John Legge, the man who devised the Poll Tax, hiding there. They were dragged out and beheaded on the spot.

Wat's peasants then moved through the city burning buildings and beheading people as they went. Some took advantage of the mayhem to loot, others to settle grudges against foreigners. Flemish immigrants bore the brunt of the rabble's anger. The rebels had an interesting way of discovering if a person was Flemish. The victim would be held down and asked to say the words 'bread and cheese'. If they pronounced it 'brod and case' they were assumed to be Flemish and their heads were cut off. (Never trust a photographer who asks you to say cheese!) Thirty-five Flemish men (or men who couldn't say bread and cheese) were beheaded outside the Church of St Martin in the Vintry near Pasternoster Lane.

Little Richard finally met one group of rebels at Mile End in East London. He agreed to all their demands. He asked them to return to their homes, leaving three representatives from each village to settle the deal. Many, believing the King's promises, left there and then.

On the sunny morning of 15 June 1381, Richard and the Lord Mayor of London, William Walworth, rode to Smithfield to meet Wat and the remaining rebels. As they approached the field they were stunned to see thousands of men waiting for them. Richard did not lose his nerve. He demanded to speak to their leader. Wat came forward. The two men shook hands. Richard calmly repeated the offer he had made at Mile End.

No one is quite sure exactly what happened next. Wat is said to have called for a flagon of beer. (Rebelling is thirsty work, after all.) This might have been to toast Richard's health on concluding their meeting. Apparently he took a single swig and then spat the foaming brew on to ground right in front of the King. William, the Mayor, was so disgusted by Wat's bad manners that he lunged forward and stabbed him with a dagger.

(In those days spitting was obviously far worse than stabbing.) Wat fell to the ground and one of the King's men finished him off by shoving a sword through his chest. In the confusion the mob could well have torn the King apart but Richard seized the moment. He declared himself their leader and asked them to follow him to Clerkenwell where he would settle their demands. Surprisingly most of them did just that. After receiving further assurances that serfdom was now ancient history they drifted away. Meanwhile Wat's head was hacked from his body and plonked on a pole on London Bridge.

The peasants were in for a shock. Richard was a lying weasel. Once the rebels were gone he changed his mind. He claimed the promises had been made under duress and were therefore worthless. To ram the point home he had his troops round up and execute anyone who had taken part in the uprising. When another rebellion broke out in Chelmsford in Essex, the teenage terror had over 500 rebels put to the sword.

Cook the cook

In 1531 one man met a truly awful but oddly appropriate death at Smithfield.

Richard Rose was the Bishop of Rochester's cook. Richard was a food fanatic. Cooking wasn't just a job for him, it was a way of life. Each day he strove to create ever more delicious dishes for Rochester and his guests. His boiled mutton was the toast of the town and neighbouring bishops used call on him on Fridays in the hope of tasting his salted salmon and turbot. Rochester held glorious lunch parties at his home in Lambeth, which often lasted from 11 in the morning until 4 o'clock in the afternoon. Richard made great platters of spiced swans, roasted geese, beef tails and quails' eggs. Rochester was particularly fond of great hearty soups flavoured with garlic and fennel. Richard spent hours simmering stock and folding in the herbs to create wonderfully satisfying broths.

A couple of days before another of Rochester's magnificent banquets, Richard was at the market buying provisions. He knew Rochester was expecting some distinguished guests and so asked Lawrence, the spice merchant, to provide him with a blend of pungent herbs to flavour the soup. Lawrence paused for a second and then produced a small jar full of dried yellow petals. Prizing off the lid, Lawrence waved the jar under Richard's nose. A beautifully spicy, sweet aroma wafted into his nostrils. These would be perfect. Richard scrabbled for his purse to pay him.

Lawrence stopped him; he made Richard swear to use only a single petal in his recipe. To use any more was dangerous. The herb was extremely potent; in small doses it was a tonic but too much of it could prove fatal. Richard promised and, after paying Lawrence, returned to Lambeth to start preparing the feast.

Richard slaved over the dishes, taking particular care with the soup. Just as his broth was thickening up he added one of the yellow petals. He waited for a few minutes and tasted his concoction. It was delicious. The petal seemed to infuse the broth with a rich nutty taste that caused his tongue to tingle with delight. Was the flavour a little too subtle? Wouldn't the soup taste even better if he added another petal? Surely one more wouldn't hurt? Lawrence was always such a worrier. Richard opened the jar and threw another petal into the pot.

Later that night the soup was served. One guest was just complimenting Rochester on its flavour when he started foaming at the mouth. Soon another guest was grovelling on floor, his hands clutching at his stomach. Eventually nineteen guests fell ill. Two later died. The soup appeared to have poisoned them. Richard was arrested and charged with their murder.

King Henry VIII, worried that his royal cooks might try the same thing, dreamt up a suitably painful punishment to fit the crime. He ordered Richard to be publicly boiled alive at

Smithfield. A huge iron cauldron, suspended on a great tripod, was set up over a pile logs. The cauldron was filled with oil and Richard, trussed up like a chicken, was thrown into it. The logs were then lit and the crowds of onlookers stood back to marvel at the sight of a man boiling in oil. It took over two hours for Richard to die. The pain must have been utterly excruciating. His death was so horrific that it was decided that in future the oil must boiled before the victim was thrown in. Thankfully the punishment was replaced with burning after Henry's death. (Out of the frying pan and into the fire!)

Flaming Fathers

It is time to return to Queen Mary I, the monarch so murderous that she was nicknamed Bloody Mary. Mary was Henry VIII's eldest daughter. Her mother, Catherine of Aragon, had raised Mary as a Catholic. Even after Henry had created the

Protestant Church of England, Mary remained loyal to her original faith. When she became Queen she reinstated Catholicism and viciously stamped out Protestant worship. Aided by Edward Bonner, her zealous Bishop of London, she had those who refused to convert to Catholicism burned to death. She only reigned for five years but in that time she had over 250 Protestants burned as heretics at Smithfield. (Her sister Elizabeth evened the score by killing the nearly the same number of Catholics during her reign. It did take her forty-five years, though!) On 29 January 1555, just four days after the Catholic Church had been restored, six men and a woman were burned to death in a single afternoon.

Haunting reminders of Mary's massacres were found in 1849. During building work fragments of charred skeletons were unearthed beside the Church of St Bartholomew-the-Great in Smithfield. The bodies appeared to have been flung into a shallow pit just outside the churchyard. There are believed to be dozens more of these pits just below the meat market. So make sure you always step carefully in Smithfield; you never know who you might be walking on.

CHAPTER FIVE

The Killing of the King

London's most famous severed head is that of King Charles I.

Charlie had never expected to be king. His older brother Henry was a bright, handsome lad whom everyone thought would make a marvellous monarch. Sadly Henry died young and so Charlie became first in line to the throne. Oh dear. Charlie really wasn't up to the job. He had been three years old before he could walk or talk. His father, James I, had suggested that cutting the end of his tongue off might help. Luckily Charlie managed to babble a few words before the doctors got the chance to perform the operation! He spoke with a stutter throughout his life. He was short, shy and had bowed legs. When Charlie became King he really did want to become a great ruler. He was simply too lazy. He enjoyed riding around in big coaches. He loved people bowing before him. He just hated having to govern the country. Did he have to spend hours every day reading and then signing all these letters and bills? Why did Parliament always moan about how much money he was spending? Why couldn't they leave him alone? All he wanted to do was play bowls and have his picture painted. What was the point of being King if you couldn't have a bit of fun?

The Government didn't agree. They regarded the king and his queen, Henrietta Maria, as indolent spendthrifts. They particularly detested the Queen. She was French and a Catholic to boot. They were convinced that she bossed Charlie about. How long, they wondered, would it be before she converted him to her faith? The palace was already spending more money on garlic, wine and cheeses. Where would it all end? The Government acted to limit Charlie's powers. Charlie was outraged. He was King. To argue with a king was to argue with God. Charlie claimed he had the divine right to rule and no earthly government could take that away from him.

The row between the King and the Houses of Parliament spiralled into a civil war. The country was split. On one side there were Royalists or Cavaliers loyal to the King, and on the other there were Roundheads or Parliamentarians - led by Oliver Cromwell - who were against the King.

The English Civil War lasted for six years but finally Oliver Cromwell's Parliamentarians were victorious. In January 1649 Charlie, who was being held at St James's Palace, was put on trial. He was accused of being a tyrant and of waging a war against his own people. Charlie refused to acknowledge the court. He argued that only God could judge a king. The court found Charlie guilty and ordered that his head should be chopped off. It was expected that the King would be beheaded at Tower Hill. Oliver was worried that someone might try to rescue the King and so arranged for him to be killed at Whitehall, which was easier to guard.

The morning of 30 January 1649 was bitterly cold. The Thames had frozen over. Charlie, worried that his shivers would be mistaken for fear, put on two shirts. His feet crunched on the icy ground as he was led across St James's Park and into Whitehall through the Holbein Gate. He must have been terrified but he showed no fear as he approached the scaffold. The state executioner had refused to kill the King. Two new men were hired. Both wore disguises as well as the usual masks. The axeman wore a huge fake beard and a grey wig. A large crowd had gathered to witness the execution.

Charlie turned to them and made a short speech denouncing the judgement. He laid his head on the block and the axeman severed it with a single blow. When the axeman held the bloody head in the air and bellowed 'Behold, the head of a traitor', the whole crowd is said to have groaned in horror.

Their horror didn't last long. After the execution the block was cut into chips and sold as souvenirs. The really ghoulish bought cloths soaked in Charlie's blood and strands of his hair. That night his body and head lay in Whitehall. For a penny you could take a look at them. Hundreds did. The next day his remains were taken to St James's Palace. His head was sewn back on to his body and the corpse was then buried at Windsor Castle.

For the next eleven years England was a king-free zone. After Oliver Cromwell's death, Parliament decided it missed having a king about the place. They asked Charlie's son, Charles, if he would like to be king. Charles, who had been living in France since his dad's execution, agreed. He had one condition. He was willing to let bygones be bygones but he could not forgive the men who had killed Charlie. He wanted those responsible executed as traitors.

There was one problem. Most of them were already dead.

So Charles had Oliver Cromwell and two of his henchmen's bodies dug up. Their festering corpses were beheaded and their heads put on display at Whitehall. A year later Oliver's head was still there. (The great London diarist Samuel Pepys recorded seeing it.) It is said to have stayed there until 1703 when a guard flogged it to tourist for a shilling (5p). No one knows where it finally ended up.

CHAPTER SIX

Nasty Newgate

Enemies of the king or queen may have enjoyed the comforts (or cruelties) of the Tower of London. Ordinary crooks were not so lucky. They were locked up in grim gaols dotted about the capital.

In medieval times a thick stone wall encircled London. The only way into the city was through gates along this wall. Aldgate, Bishopsgate and Newgate are all old gateways. These gates were like little castles, with their own armouries and dungeons. Shifty-looking characters could be kept out of the city and wrongdoers trying to escape were kept in. As the city grew, some of these gatehouses became proper prisons. The largest and most gruesome was Newgate. From the 1100s until 1903 - when it was finally demolished - this filthy gaol stood where the Old Bailey - our largest law courts - are today.

Newgate was such a disgustingly smelly prison that it made passers-by puke. Its water supply was so polluted that rats swam in it. A putrid foul fog hung over the whole place. Gaol fever - a horrible disease like Typhoid - was rife. Hundreds of prisoners awaiting the death sentence actually died before the hangman got the chance to kill them! In 1414 forty prisoners and the gaoler died of gaol fever in one single week.

New prisoners were prodded into the gaol by guards with pitchforks. Once inside they had to pay an entrance fee to the gaolers. The keeper - the prison's chief - and his gaolers earned their wages from the fees they charged prisoners. The more the prisoners paid the better they were treated. If you had money, a comfortable cell and all the luxuries of the outside world could be yours.

Those with no cash soon found themselves stripped of their clothes and loaded with chains. In 1290 one man was chained so heavily his spine snapped. (Backbreaking work for the guards!) Forty years later the keeper Edmund le Lorimer was himself gaoled for mercilessly chaining his prisoners. Guards also bullied, robbed and tortured convicts to top up their pay packets. (Apart from the really nasty ones who did it for fun.)

Newgate Gaol: Chaining People Is Our Game

Guards Wanted!

Are you a misshapen thug? Do you like hurting people? Love dungeons? Ever thought of becoming a prison guard?

We are currently looking for enthusiastic, unpleasant people to join our team.

We offer a generous salary and a great bonus scheme

Our perks:

• A snazzy sackcloth uniform

• Your own pitchfork

You must be:

- Aggressive, cruel and greedy

- Fond of taking bribes

- Able to use locks and keys

- A good team torturer

- Excellent at shouting

- Willing to work long hours in a dark, smelly hole

No previous experience required, but having warts and not being able to recall the last time you had a bath an advantage.

Apply in person to:

The Keeper
Newgate Gaol
Newgate St
London
EC4

Newgate Gaol is an evil opportunities employer

The most unfortunate (normally the poorest) inmates were cast into Newgate's horrific underground dungeons. These cells were in complete darkness and absolutely filthy. There were no beds, only damp stone floors scattered with straw. The straw was infested with lice, which you may have already discovered for yourself are disgusting insects. The lice cracked and squished like eggshells as the prisoners shuffled about.

Food was scarce. The guards occasionally threw pieces of stale bread into the cells. The prisoners then had to scrabble around on the floor, fighting with the rats and each other, for these pitiful scraps. The starving tried to eat dead rats or shoved lice into their mouths. (Medieval sushi, anyone?)

Things were not much better in other parts of the prison. Blankets and even beds could be hired and candles could be bought but conditions were still dirty and squalid. Those with enough money could block out the horrors by getting drunk. Beer and gin were cheap and readily available. Keepers encouraged drinking because they made huge profits on the sale of booze.

Keepers didn't have it all their own way. Many of the prisoners were violent and unruly. Breakouts were common and in 1325 a gang of prisoners murdered three guards and the keeper while making their escape.

Newgate wasn't all doom and gloom. Wives and whole families lived in the prison. Accommodation was mixed until the Victorian times. Parts of the prison were more like a bad disco than a prison. Inmates could drink, dance and flirt their days away. Until 1792 pets, pigs and pigeons could also be kept in the cells.

Most prisoners didn't spend more than few weeks in Newgate. Criminals were only kept there until their trials. If they were found innocent they were instantly released. The guilty were taken back to gaol until they could be executed. Debtors - people who owed money - were held for longer. They were imprisoned until their creditors were satisfied. Some who'd paid off their debts couldn't then afford to pay the guards the required leaving fee. They remained trapped in the prison for the rest of their lives. In 1689 a military man, Major John Bernardi, was imprisoned in Newgate. Somehow his case was completely forgotten about and he died forty-seven years later, still awaiting a trial! During his time inside he and his wife had ten children.

Pressed to Death

Until 1828 anyone who flatly refused to say whether they had committed a crime or not faced a dreadful torture. The prisoner was chained to the floor and heavy weights were plonked on their chest. More weights were added until the victim either agreed to speak or died when their rib cage caved in. This nasty punishment was politely called the *peine forte et dure* (a strong and slow torture.). Newgate had a whole yard for pressing. (They worked flat out!)

Many visitors to the prison were themselves criminals. They popped in to visit old friends and even to buy and sell stolen goods. Newgate was the nerve centre of London's criminal underworld. From inside its walls daring robberies and escapes were planned. Young criminals learned how to pick pockets, carry out burglaries and even how to forge coins. Newgate was London's college of crime!

Newgate College of Crime

It is hereby certified that:

Johnny 'Light Fingers' Smith is now a fully qualified crook.

During his time at Newgate he has learned how to Pick Pockets and Break into Houses

16th March 1671

Signed

Dick Spraggot
Master Burgler

LONDON PRISONS
– THE TERRIBLE TOP FIVE

Newgate was the worst; how bad were the others?

The Clink, Southwark

It is now a great gruesome museum but did you know that it gave us the phrase 'in the clink', meaning to be in prison?

In 1761 it was described as 'a very dismal hole.'

The Fleet, Farringdon

The Fleet was a real fire hazard. It burned to the ground in 1666 in the Great Fire of London and again in 1780!

Life in the Fleet was depicted by the writer Charles Dickens in his book *The Pickwick Papers*.

In 1691 one prisoner, Moses Pitt, said that prisoners 'pick'd lice off their outer garments' ...

Clerkenwell Bridewell House of Detention – New Prison.

Clerkenwell is also now a museum but it was once London's most vicious prison - offenders were punished by being beaten up or whipped. The London artist William Hogarth painted grim goings-on there.

Marshalsea, Southwark

The father of writer Charles Dickens was imprisoned here!

Charles described it in his book *Little Dorrit* as 'a pile ... of squalid houses'.

Coldbath Fields Prison, Farringdon

Coldbath Fields was so strict that the poets Robert Southey and Samuel Taylor Coleridge wrote a poem about it called 'The Devil's Thoughts':

As he went through Cold Bath Fields he saw
A solitary cell;
And the Devil was pleased, for it gave him a hint
For improving his prisons Hell.

Gorblimey Gordon

A few years later Lord George Gordon's mob didn't stage a prison breakout; they broke up the entire gaol!

Lord George Gordon detested Catholics. As far as he was concerned the only good Catholic was a dead one. He hated them so much that he would break into violent rages if the name of the Pope - the head of the Catholic Church - was even mentioned in his company. In 1778 the Government had passed a new 'let's be nice to Catholics' law. Gordon was furious. He was so angry that he mounted a campaign to get the law changed. He wrote to the newspapers, he called for debates in Parliament and he ranted at just about anyone who would listen. After two years of getting nowhere, he took more radical action. On 4 June 1780 he led an armed mob to the Houses of Parliament. After presenting a petition to Parliament, the mob went on the rampage across the city. For the next five days a full-scale riot raged through London's streets. It was the biggest public disturbance since Wat Tyler's Peasant Revolt.

By 6 June 1780 the mob had made their way to Newgate Gaol. They demanded to speak to the keeper, Richard Akerman.

Richard had been about to tuck into his supper. His cook had prepared a plate of boiled beef and carrots and he was looking forward to washing it down with a glass of port. The last thing he wanted or needed was an angry mob at the gates. The prisoners inside were bad enough.

'Good evening, gentlemen, and what can I do for you?' said
Richard, leaning out of an upper-floor window.

'Mr Keeper, you have some of our friends in your prison,' said
the mob.

Glancing down at the grubby mass below he was not surprised.
What an ugly-looking lot they were.

'Look, lads, I'm an awfully busy man. I've got a lot of people in
this prison. Can you be more specific?'

'Damn you, keeper! Open the gates or we'll burn you down and
let everyone out,' was the mob's somewhat terse reply.

Charming, thought Richard. You try and talk to these people
like they're decent human beings and see what you get. Let them
stew. They'll probably get bored and wander off, with any luck.

They didn't. Richard was forced to flee when the rabble
broke into his house and set fire to it. The mob then started a
fire at main door. It wasn't long before the door was ablaze.
Burning torches were thrown on to the roof and the fire spread
throughout the prison. (One enterprising neighbour charged
spectators sixpence each to watch the inferno from his roof.) A

set of keys was seized from a terrified guard and they set about opening the cells. By the end of the night over 300 prisoners had been freed. The prison had been reduced to a smouldering shell.

The next day some of the prisoners, after years in Newgate, were unable to cope with the outside world. They wandered back to the glowing ruins. A few even lay down in the rubble where their cells had once been.

The rioting lasted for another three days. Nearby Fleet Prison and the Clink in Southwark were also burnt to the ground. Nearly 500 people were killed or wounded in the turmoil. The mob ran out of steam after Gordon was arrested. He was taken to the Tower of London. (It had not been burnt down.) The terror was over.

Gordon escaped the clutches of the hangman (thirty-five other rioters were not so lucky) and was eventually given a prison sentence. Guess where he was banged up? Yes, it was Newgate. It was quickly rebuilt and Gordon found himself lodged in the very prison his mob had destroyed. Gordon was fortunate enough to have pots of cash; no hideous hovel for him. He paid for the best cell in the prison. He had his own servants and he even held a dinner party every fortnight.

His wealth, however, didn't protect him from Newgate's dreaded gaol fever. He died of the disease in 1793.

CHAPTER SEVEN

The Golden Age of the Gallows

Until the reign of Queen Victoria, the most common punishment for stealing was death by hanging. There were gallows all over London – at Blackheath, Kennington Common, Bloomsbury Square, Soho Square, Smithfield, St Giles in Holborn and on City Road in Islington. You could hardly move for swinging bodies. The trendiest place to die was Tyburn - now the site of Marble Arch, then on the very edge of London. From the 1400s until 1783 most of London's criminals were strung up there.

The first execution at Tyburn took place in 1196. The victim was William 'Longbeard' Fitzosbert.

Bill the Beard

The King of the day, Richard the Lionheart, spent more time fighting in the Crusades - a bloody war in the Holy Land between Christians, Muslims and Jews - than he did ruling England. (In fact, Richard was only in England for six months of his entire reign!) In 1193 he was on his way back to England after a fine time slaughtering in the Third Crusade when he managed to get himself captured by King Henry of Austria. Henry, keen to bolster his royal purse, held Richard for a (king's) ransom - he wanted money and lots of it before he'd return Richard to England.

The only way to raise the ransom was to increase taxes. After three years of being taxed to the hilt the English were a bit fed up with paying for their absent king. The Londoner William 'Longbeard' Fitzosbert felt the taxes were far too high. He led a public rebellion against them in the capital. The rebellion was quashed and Bill the Beard fled into the Church of St Mary-le-Bow in the heart of the city. Churches were then places of sanctuary. As long as Bill stayed inside the church he couldn't be arrested. The men sent to apprehend him were so annoyed they set fire to the church. When the smoke poured in, Bill came stumbling out. He was dragged off to Tyburn and hanged.

We have no record of the numbers of people hanged at Tyburn over the next couple of hundred years. Early historians weren't too bothered about how ordinary criminals died. Like newspapers and magazines now, they were more interested in famous people. There were always plenty of traitors, spies and bishops being executed at the Tower and Smithfield to write about.

In the 1400s - during the reign of King Henry IV - Tyburn was well known as a place of public execution. The first permanent gallows were built 1571. Tyburn's triangular gallows were constructed to execute John Story, a Catholic doctor, whom Queen Elizabeth I had taken a dislike to. Nicknamed the Triple Tree, these gallows had three legs and three beams - a bit like a camera tripod or a giant wooden Toblerone on its side. Each beam could hold eight people. This meant the hangman could kill a staggering twenty-four people in one go! The device was so notorious that by 1595 Willliam Shakespeare put it in his play, *Love Labour's Lost*.

Thous mak'st the triumviry,
The corner of society.
The shape of Love's Tyburn,
That hangs up simplicity.

(They are not his best lines but you try getting mass slaughter into a romantic comedy.)

During the reign of King James I about 150 people were hanged at Tyburn each year. By the 1700s, the Government had become worried about rising crime. They decided to deter wrongdoers by making even more crimes punishable by death. This didn't stop crime; they just had to execute more people. It was not uncommon for forty or more to hang in a single day. Most of the criminals executed were under twenty-one years of age and had stolen goods worth less than a pound. In 1720 over 200 crimes carried the death sentence.

You could be executed for some very odd things:

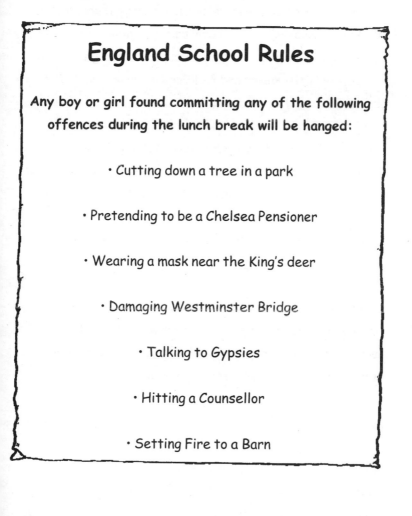

England School Rules

Any boy or girl found committing any of the following offences during the lunch break will be hanged:

· Cutting down a tree in a park

· Pretending to be a Chelsea Pensioner

· Wearing a mask near the King's deer

· Damaging Westminster Bridge

· Talking to Gypsies

· Hitting a Counsellor

· Setting Fire to a Barn

For the very poor life was hard enough as it was. London was cramped, dirty and disease-ridden. (No change there, then!) Work was backbreaking and badly paid. (Er, ditto.) If you could be hanged for stealing a single silver spoon, you might as well make off with the knives and forks and be done with it. The punishment was the same: death.

As a highwayman in a book by Daniel Defoe - the author of *Robinson Crusoe* - says, 'at the place of execution there at least was an End of all the Miseries of the present State.'

It was better to live fast and die young than live miserably and, well ... still die young.

Hangings were held every six weeks at Tyburn. These Hangings Days were public holidays - it was hoped the sight of a hanging would deter crime. The atmosphere, however, was usually more like a carnival than a funeral.

The Tyburn trail

The journey to the gallows was like a lap of honour for the condemned. Although it was only a few miles from Newgate Prison to Tyburn the procession could take hours. Huge crowds blocked the streets. Girls wore their best white dresses and showered dashing young villains with flowers. The victims often dressed in their finest clothes. In 1750, the dandy highwayman

72

John Maclean went to his death dressed in a snazzy silk waistcoat and a pair of yellow slippers. (He was a fashion victim!) People drank and danced along the way. There were sellers of gingerbread, gin and oranges. It was like going to watch a football match; there were songs and chants, programmes and banners.

The journey wasn't quite so fun for nasty murderers or those who had annoyed the public; they were pelted with rotten vegetables and stones.

The condemned were taken in a horse-drawn cart from Newgate to the Church of St Sepulchre, where a bell was tolled and they were given a bunch of posies. They then rolled along through Smithfield and up into Holborn. At the Church of St Giles-in-the-Fields the cart stopped for jugs of ale. The Bowl Inn at St Giles and the White Heart on Drury Lane were also popular pit stops. Many were blind drunk by the time they reached the gallows. After Holborn the cart trundled up into the edges of Soho and on to Oxford Road (now Oxford Street) and finally arrived at Tyburn itself.

The trip to Tyburn roughly follows the Central Line of the modern London Underground:

St Pauls--Chancery Lane--Holborn--Tottenham Court Road--Oxford St--Bond St--Marble Arch

Rich and poor all flocked to the hangings. Public executions were London's most popular spectator sport. (People were simply dying to watch them!) Around the gallows were wooden galleries, like those at a racetrack, where spectators paid 2 shillings (10p) for a good view. The largest stand - with the best views - was known as Old Mother Proctor's Pews (after the woman who owned it and surprise, surprise, because they looked a bit like church pews.) The wealthy hired windows and balconies overlooking the scaffold. Before the executions the keeper of Newgate prison entertained distinguished guests by giving them a lavish breakfast of devilled kidneys and brandy.

The cart was pulled up directly under the gallows. A priest, called an Ordinary (though he did have an odd job), gave a prayer and asked the condemned to apologize for their crimes. Some gave long speeches to the crowd, others used the moment to insult their captors or the priest. The priests were also at risk from the hangmen. On one occasion a drunken hangman slung a rope over the priest's head as he was bent in prayer.

Once the nooses were in place, the hangman whipped the horses so that the cart flew off leaving the condemned to dangle until they died. This could take ages. As they kicked, convulsing and gasping for breath, friends and relatives

would tug on their legs to help speed things up. (Never! You're pulling my leg.)

When death finally came the bodies were cut down. The hangman was entitled to keep the corpses and their clothes. (In 1447 five men were stripped and prepared for hanging when their pardons arrived. The hangman refused to give them back their clothes. They had to walk home naked. Still, better than being dead!) If the victim's family wanted the body they had to buy it from the hangman. In the 1700s the hangman could also sell bodies to doctors and surgeons for grisly medical experiments.

Dead bodies were thought to have magical powers. To touch a corpse straight off the gallows was supposed to be good luck. (What was wrong with a horseshoe?) Scuffles would break out between the family of the dead, those trying to lay their grubby mitts on the corpse and the surgeons, who wanted to drag the body away and start slicing it up. In the confusion bodies were sometimes snatched and later sold to shifty surgeons on the sly.

Hanging wasn't good enough for John Haynes. His body was taken to a surgeon for dissection. Before the surgeon had the chance to get his scalpel out, John woke up. He remembered not a jot about his hanging. The last thing he could recall was being driven through Holborn in the cart.

After the whole ghastly spectacle was over the executioner would make his way to a pub in Fleet Street and sell bits of rope as souvenirs.

Clumsy Ketch

The most hopeless hangman of all time was Jack Ketch.

Richard Jaquet was known as Jack Ketch to his friends, enemies and just about everyone, really. (Only his mum still called him Richard.) He wasn't the first public executioner but he was certainly the worst. After him, all hangmen were nicknamed Jack Ketch. Even the puppet hangman in Punch and Judy shows bears his name.

One of Jack's predecessors had been Derrick the Dab-handed. Derrick had taken the job very seriously. Derrick had dreamt up new knots and twiddled with the shape of the gallows to make it more efficient. Like a professional golfer he had spent hours practising with his axe. Derrick had been able to sever most heads with a single blow. People had feared Derrick but they had respected his work. Derrick was a killing craftsman, an execution artist. Slipping Derrick a gold coin or a bit extra as you approached the block or scaffold secured a swift and easy exit. Derrick hadn't thought of these payments as bribes; they were tributes to his skill as a professional. They had paid him because they trusted him to do a good job. Barbers and hairdressers got tips for good work, why shouldn't he?

Jack, on the other hand, was a clumsy bungler. He tried to do a good job, he really did, but he just wasn't up to it. No matter how many hours he spent practising with his nooses or playing with his axe he still couldn't get it right. The more mistakes he made the more the crowd laughed and insulted him. How was he supposed to work with a mob braying for his blood? It disturbed his concentration. The criminals all got killed in the end. Why did it matter if it took a bit longer or if hurt them a bit more? This was execution – it wasn't meant to be fun! Things reached a head (sorry about the pun) in July 1683 when he executed Lord William Russell.

William had got himself tangled up in a plot to kill King Charles II. Charles had responded by sentencing him to death. William paid Jack 20 guineas (gold coins) to do the job swiftly.

On the day of the execution William laid his head on the block and waited for the fatal blow. Jack raised the axe. The crowd gasped. The axe hurtled down but only glanced the side of William's neck. Jack had botched it. William was furious. He is reported to have bellowed:

'You dog! Did I pay you to treat me so inhumanly?'

It took Jack three blows to sever his head. (Third time lucky.) Jack was jeered as he walked away.

Live from the Chopping Match we speak to Jack Ketch

Reporter: Hello, ladies and gentlemen, you join us live from Lincoln's Inn Fields in Holborn, London. Jack Ketch has just come off the pitch after executing Lord William Russell. We are hoping to get a few words with him. Ah ... here he is. Jack, what did you think of your performance today?

Jack: Well, Ron, I'll be honest. I felt my axe control slipped a bit in the first half but at the end of the day I think the result speaks for itself.

Rep: Some felt that you were a bit clumsy. The diarist Big John Evelyn described your chopping as 'barbarous'.

Jack: No! No, Ron, I was not clumsy. Big John may know a thing or two about trees and Tenerife but he still has a lot to learn about executions. I wasn't as tidy as I could have been but I felt my second chop was spot on.

Rep: And your third?

Jack:A nifty little follow-through, didn't you think?

Rep: Er … It looked to me as if you were covering up for fluffing the first two.

Jack: No! No! No, Ron. All part of my game plan.

Rep: Commentators have contrasted your, shall we say, more relaxed style with that of Dab-hand Derrick's. How do you think you differ?

Jack: I have nothing but respect for Derrick but I just feel that my fluid style suits the modern game. People like an executioner who's willing to go for the hard tackles. You know, taking the man down and worrying about the niceties later. They want results and I am just the man for the job.

Rep: Yes, Jack, but there have been a few occasions this season when the score sheet hasn't looked so good.

Jack: Look, Ron you're not going to bring up that noose business again, are you? I tied those knots perfectly. It was the rope that failed. So what if it took them a quarter of an hour or more to die? I'm giving the public value for money.

Rep: There have been calls for you to resign. How do you feel about that?

Jak: Rather hurt, Ron. I can honestly say I've given it 100% this season.

Rep: Thanks, Jack. That's all from me at Lincoln's Inn Fields. Now it's back to Southwark for bear-baiting with Des.

Two years later Jack made a complete mess of the Duke of Monmouth's execution. The Duke was taken to Tower Hill for beheading. After four blows, the Duke's head still clung to his shoulders. Jack slung the axe aside and grabbed a knife. He sliced at the neck as if it was were a loaf of bread until finally the stubborn head fell to the floor with a bump.

In 1686 Jack got into an argument with one of the city sheriffs and was sacked. A man called Pascha Rose replaced him. Pascha had been a meat butcher and was by all accounts a very nasty piece of work. After only a few months in the job he was arrested for murder and was himself hanged at Tyburn in June 1686. Jack got his old job back. He didn't get to enjoy it for long; he died three months later. Few missed him. His wife, however, always maintained that only her beloved Jack had known how to 'make men die sweetly.' (Um ... I'm not sure the Duke of Monmouth would have agreed!)

All hung up

In 1752 the Government decided that the bodies of the most notorious crooks – such as highwaymen – wouldn't be buried or even dissected. Instead they would be put on display to serve as a warning to others.

Putting bodies on show wasn't a new thing – London Bridge had been cluttered with severed heads for centuries - but it is shocking to think that this was made legal only a couple of years before the British Museum in Bloomsbury opened and the first English dictionary was published.

After being hanged the bodies of these criminals were thrown into a cauldron of boiling pitch – a foul sticky mixture normally used on roofs. Once the bodies were completely coated they were fished out and wrapped in chains. This wasn't to stop them escaping (it was too late for that!) – the chains were used to secure the corpses to posts. These posts were called 'gibbets'.

These gibbets were usually placed on the main roads into the city – the very same roads plagued by robbers and highwaymen. (Some deterrent!) There were gibbets in Kensington and Knightsbridge, now posh parts of town but then villages on the outskirts of the city. Highgate, Hampstead and Finchley in the north and Wimbledon and Putney in the south all had gibbets. While today we have signs welcoming visitors to London, travellers in days gone were greeted by rotting bodies, swinging in chains. (One hell of a welcome!) This grim practice was finally abolished in 1834.

The Thief-Finder

When things are stolen, rewards for the return of property or the arrest of the thief are sometimes offered. In the 1720s this was very common. There was still no proper police force. Judges and magistrates offered rewards to encourage people to turn in wrongdoers. One man who took advantage of this system was Jonathan Wild.

Jonathan's scam was to offer to find stolen goods and capture crooks. He called himself the Thief-Taker. The government and rich members of the public, desperate to tackle crime, eagerly sought his help. His success rate was impressive. He sent sixty-seven crooks to the gallows and recovered thousands of items. He himself made a small fortune in rewards. What was the secret of his success? Jonathan was really the Godfather of London's criminal underworld. A bit like Fagin in *Oliver Twist* he ran a huge network of pickpockets, thieves and highwaymen. He could usually get stolen goods back because one of his men had nicked them. Crooks who refused to play ball or were no longer of use to him he had hanged.

Eventually the government uncovered Jonathan's devious scheme and arrested him for selling stolen goods. The thief-taker was exposed as a thief and sent to Tyburn.

There were no flowers or dancing girls for Jonathan. He was pelted with rotted eggs and rancid fruit all the way to the gallows. The mob cheered when the noose was put around his next and roared with laughter when the hangman drove the cart away.

Ta ta to Tyburn

By the 1780s, the procession to Tyburn had become a farce. Pickpockets stole in the shadows of the gallows. Tyburn, once an out-of-the-way swamp, was now a little too close to the new fashionable West End. Hanging was out, shopping was in. Public hangings were ended at Tyburn in 1783. The gallows were moved to Newgate Prison. The gingerbread, gin and orange-sellers weren't the only ones annoyed by the change.

Dr Samuel Johnson – one of London's greatest writers but a bit of a smelly old grouch – was flabbergasted: 'The age is running mad after change,' he grumbled. 'Tyburn itself is not safe from the fury of innovation ... The old method was most satisfactory to all parties; the publick was gratified by the procession; the criminal supported by it. Why is all this to be swept away?'

Progress, perhaps?

Chapter Eight

Ready for Reform

Tyburn wasn't the only thing changing. As the 1700s drew to a close there were new ideas about how to deal with crime and how to punish wrongdoers.

From Bow Street Boys to Bobbies

For 600 hundred years, London had no police force. Like our Neighbourhood Watch schemes today people just kept an eye on each other. Each borough or street had a team of nosy parkers who patrolled the streets at night. Not many people wanted to do this. It was dark, dangerous and there were crooks about. The job usually fell to doddery old men who were useless at catching wrongdoers.

In 1748 the writer Henry Fielding was appointed as a magistrate (a minor judge) at Bow St Law Courts. He was so appalled by the corrupt and clumsy clods who patrolled the city that he sacked them. He found six men he trusted and gave them jobs as constables. These Bow St Runners, as they were called, were London's first proper police force. Henry wrote to the Government demanding money to fund his policing schemes. He published a book called *Enquiries into the Causes of the Late Increase in Robberies* about how he planned to tackle crime. He knocked on doors, banged on tables and generally created such a fuss that he got enough cash to get his Runners running.

The Bow St Runners were amazingly successful. Within a few weeks they had arrested a gang of horrible highwaymen who had terrorized the roads into town. The government was so impressed that it paid for a squad of ten men at Bow St. When Henry died in 1754 his blind brother John took over. John 'the blind beak' was just as determined as Henry to stamp out crooks. He set up night patrols on the turnpikes - the gates - into the city. The numbers of highway robberies fell dramatically. The government, convinced that the problem was over, refused to give John any more cash. John was livid. He had to stop the patrols. The crafty highwaymen, spotting the coast was clear, returned in droves. By the 1770s things were as bad as before and yet the government still refused to pay for a police force.

The government finally came to its senses in 1805 and the patrols returned. In 1829 the government's Home Secretary (the person in charge of law and order), Sir Robert Peel, expanded the patrol to form a new police force for the whole of London - from Highgate in the north to Camberwell in the south. The Metropolitan Police – nicknamed Peelers or Bobbies after its founder – has protected London ever since.

Cruikshank's Cartoon

George Cruikshank was an artist and cartoonist who illustrated many of Charles Dickens's books. One spring morning in 1818 he was strolling down Ludgate Hill near St Paul's cathedral. It was early, about half-past eight. George was not quite awake yet. His arms and legs moved steadily along but his mind drifted. He thought about buying some new charcoals; he thought about what he was going to have for his lunch and even how much nicer it would be to be safely tucked up in bed again. His thoughts were rudely interrupted when he came face to face with a gallows strewn with dead bodies. Two of the bodies were young women who looked barely older than sixteen. He was deeply shocked. He asked a man nearby what they had been hanged for. He discovered the girls had been caught trying to use a forged £1 note (the old paper version of a pound coin). George was heartbroken that they had lost their lives over such a tiny sum of money.

He was determined to put a stop to this. He sketched his own £1 note. Instead of the head of the Queen his note featured a row of corpses swinging from ropes. When his sketch was published it caused an outrage. The Bank of England even had to stop issuing pound notes for a time. Stunned members of the public called for a change in the law. The Home Secretary – good old Robert 'Police Bobby' Peel – eventually bowed to public pressure and abolished the death penalty for minor crimes in 1832. George's cartoon had ended nearly 700 years of senseless killing.

The end is nigh

In 1868 the gruesome spectacle of public executions finished. The last public hanging was held outside Newgate Prison on 26 May 1868. The victim was a terrorist called Michael Barratt who had blown up the Clerkenwell House of Detention, killing six people.

In the 1820s a bold young woman called Elizabeth Fry had led a campaign to improve conditions in prisons. Her enterprising work resulted in cleaner cells and a school being set up in Newgate. In 1823 a 'let's have some nicer prisons' act was passed, based on Elizabeth's ideas. Queen Victoria's London saw new, modern prisons being built, many of which are still in use today. Wandsworth, Pentonville and Holloway were all built in the 1840s and 1850s. The age of grim dungeons was over.

The gallows carried on until 1965, when the death penalty was finally abolished. Pirates and traitors could still be hanged but in 1999 Parliament eventually removed the death penalty from English law. After over 1000 years capital punishment had finally got the chop. Hurrah!

Here are some gruesome things to do to while away some rainy days. For more inspiration, look at some of the places you can visit on pages 93–94.

IMAGINE

... you're in Newgate Gaol. You stole a loaf of bread because you were hungry and poor, and now you're awaiting trial. Write a letter to your best friend, describing the prison, the guards and your fellow prisoners.

... you're one of the Princes in the Tower and you escaped after all. You've decided to write to a major newspaper revealing your identity. What happened? And what disguise did you adopt? And was Uncle Richard as bad as they all said he was?

... you're Queen Elizabeth I and you have to sign a death warrant for the execution of someone you were fond of but who betrayed you. What would your diary for that day say?

... you're William the Conqueror and you're designing your new dream Tower of London. What would you put in it and why? Draw a plan.

... you're one of London's first police officers. How will people treat you? What things will you have to change? Write out what you think would be a job description.

QUIZ

See if you can remember some gory facts

1) What did the Romans call London?

_____

2) On what day of the year was William the Conqueror
crowned King of England?

_____

3) Which king built the Tower of London?

_____

4) What was the punishment of choice for nobles in the
Middle Ages?

_____

5) Which monarch invented the gruesome punishment of hanging, drawing and quartering?

_____

6) Which king had 70,000 people executed during his reign?

_____

7) What was the nickname of Queen Mary, Henry VIII's eldest daughter?

_____

8) What was Wat Tyler's profession? If you can't remember, have a guess – there's a clue.

_____

9) Which monarch literally lost his head?

_____

10) When was London's first official police force founded?

_____

See overleaf for the answers

Answers

1) Londinium
2) Christmas Day
3) William the Conqueror
4) Beheading
5) Henry III
6) Henry VIII
7) Bloody Mary
8) He was a roofer
9) Charles I
10) 1829

Gory Places to Visit

The Chamber of Horrors, Madame Tussauds, Marylebone Road, London NW1. Although never a real torture chamber, the spooky Chamber has plenty of grisly exhibits. www.madame-tussauds.com

The City of London Police, Black Museum, New Scotland Yard, London SW1, houses a grim array of murder weapons. www.met.police.uk

The Clerkenwell House of Detention, Clerkenwell Close, London EC1, is fantastic. This vast underground museum gives a frightening taste of the gruesome reality of prison life.

The Clink Prison Museum, 1 Clink Street, London SE1. The museum of the prison 'that gave its name to all others', has a delightful collection of torture devices. www.clink.co.uk

Dickens House Museum, 48 Doughty Street, London WC1. Charles Dickens's house has been preserved as it was in the 1830s. It is full of his possessions, including bars from Marshalsea Prison where his father was locked up for debt. www.dickensmuseum.com

The Jewish Museum, 129-131 Albert St, Camden, London NW1, has a wealth of information on London's Jewish History. www.jewmusm.ort.org

The London Dungeon, 28-34 Tooley St, London SE1, is London's most terrifying tourist spot. Explore grim torture chambers, watch horrible executions, trail Jack the Ripper's gruesome murders, come face to face with foul figures from the past and even get sentenced to death! www.thedungeons.com

The Old Bailey Law Courts, Old Bailey, London EC1. Newgate Gaol was knocked down in 1902 but a blue plaque commemorates the spot.

The Museum of London, at 150 London Wall, London, EC2 has a re-creation of a typical Newgate cell (though thankfully not the smell). The museum is packed full of interesting stuff on London. www.museum-london.org.uk

The skeleton of London's criminal mastermind, Jonathan Wild, is on display at the **Museum of the Royal College of Surgeons**, 35-43 Lincoln's Inn Fields, London WC2.
They also have a fantastic collection of horrible surgical instruments from 1700s-1900s. You'll also find the Hunterian Museum here. www.rcseng.ac.uk

The Old Operating Theatre, Museum and Herb Garret, 9a St Thomas's Street, London SE1, has a reconstruction of an old surgery – just the sort of place where criminals like John Haynes were taken to be dissected. www.thegarrett.org.uk

The Tower of London, Tower Hill, London EC3, royal palace, prison and place of execution is a top spot to visit. The Yeoman Guards – nicknamed Beefeaters – give wonderful tours and they will even show you the very spot where poor old Anne Boleyn had her head chopped off. www.toweroflondontour.com

The Tyburn Plaque, at the junction of Edgware and Bayswater Rd, Marble Arch. The gallows have long gone but a plaque marks the spot where they used to stand. (It is quite hard to find, though.)

The Original London Walk, P.O. Box 1708, London, NW6 4LW. This company run loads of great walks around the city. www.walks.com

If you enjoyed this book, why not try others in the series:

CRYPTS, CAVES AND TUNNELS OF LONDON
by Ian Marchant
Peel away the layers under your feet and discover
the unseen treasures of London beneath the streets.
ISBN 1-904153-04-6

GRAVE-ROBBERS, CUT-THROATS AND POISONERS
OF LONDON
by Helen Smith
Dive into London's criminal past and meet some of its
thieves, murderers and villains.
ISBN 1-904153-00-3

RATS, BATS, FROGS AND BOGS OF LONDON
by Chris McLaren
Find out where you can find some of the amazing species
London has to offer the budding naturalist.
ISBN 1-904153-05-4

THE BLACK DEATH AND OTHER PLAGUES OF LONDON
by Natasha Narayan
Read about some of the most vile and rampant diseases ever
known
and how Londoners overcame them – or not!
ISBN 1-904153-01-1

GHOSTS, GHOULS AND PHANTOMS OF LONDON
by Travis Elborough
Meet some of the victims of London's bloodthirsty monarchs,
murderers, plagues, fires and famines - who've chosen to stick
around!
ISBN 1-904153-02-X

In case you have difficulty finding any Watling St books in your local bookshop, you can place orders directly through

BOOKPOST
Freepost
PO Box 29
Douglas
Isle of Man
IM99 1BQ

Telephone: 01624 836000
e-mail: bookshop@enterprise.net